Este es el Sol

Escrito por **Elizabeth Everett**

Ilustrado por **Evelline Andrya**

Science, Naturally!
Un sello de Platypus Media, LLC

Este es el **Sol.**

Esta es la **luz** del Sol.

Este es el **árbol** que hace su comida con la luz del Sol.

Esta es la **flor** que empieza a brotar creciendo en el árbol

que hace su comida con la luz del Sol.

Este es el **bicho** que se sienta en la hoja y come la flor

que empieza a brotar creciendo en el árbol
que hace su comida con la luz del Sol.

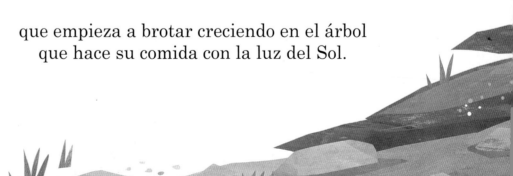

Esta es la **araña** que teje su tela para atrapar al bicho

que se sienta en la hoja y come la flor
que empieza a brotar creciendo en el árbol
que hace su comida con la luz del Sol.

Esta es la **iguana** que lanza su lengua y apresa a la araña

que teje su tela para atrapar al bicho
que se sienta en la hoja y come la flor
que empieza a brotar creciendo en el árbol
que hace su comida con la luz del Sol.

Esta es la **serpiente** que abre su boca y caza a la iguana

que lanza su lengua y apresa a la araña
que teje su tela para atrapar al bicho
que se sienta en la hoja y come la flor
que empieza a brotar creciendo en el árbol
que hace su comida con la luz del Sol.

Esta es la **zorra** que callada acecha a la incauta serpiente

que abre su boca y caza a la iguana
que lanza su lengua y apresa a la araña
que teje su tela para atrapar al bicho
que se sienta en la hoja y come la flor
que empieza a brotar creciendo en el árbol
que hace su comida con la luz del Sol.

Esta es la **caca** que cayó al suelo a los pies de la zorra

que callada acecha a la incauta serpiente
que abre su boca y caza a la iguana
que lanza su lengua y apresa a la araña
que teje su tela para atrapar al bicho
que se sienta en la hoja y come la flor
que empieza a brotar creciendo en el árbol
que hace su comida con la luz del Sol.

Esta es la **semilla** que viene del árbol y cae en la caca

que cayó al suelo a los pies de la zorra
que callada acecha a la incauta serpiente
que abre su boca y caza a la iguana
que lanza su lengua y apresa a la araña
que teje su tela para atrapar al bicho
que se sienta en la hoja y come la flor
que empieza a brotar creciendo en el árbol
que hace su comida con la luz del Sol.

Este es el **brote**
que crece de la semilla
y se orienta al Sol...

y este es el **Sol**
que genera este ciclo de vida.

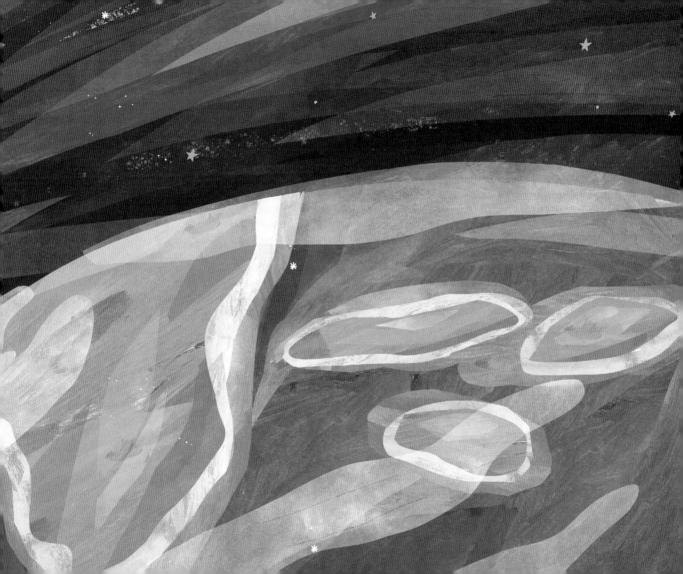

¡Ahora voltea este libro para leerlo en inglés!

Now flip this book over to read it in Spanish!

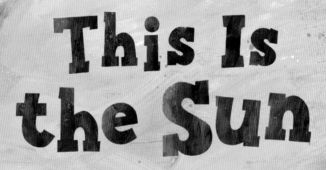

This Is the Sun

Written *by* **Elizabeth Everett**
Illustrated *by* **Evelline Andrya**

Science, Naturally!
An imprint of Platypus Media, LLC

This is the **Sun.**

This is the **light**
that comes from the Sun.

This is the **tree** that uses the light from the Sun to make its own food.

This is the **flower** that starts to bloom as it grows on the tree

that uses the light from the Sun to make its own food.

This is the **bug** that sits on a leaf and nibbles the flower

that starts to bloom as it grows on the tree
that uses the light from the Sun to make its own food.

This is the **spider** that spins its web to trap the bug

that sits on a leaf and nibbles the flower
that starts to bloom as it grows on the tree
that uses the light from the Sun to make its own food.

This is the **lizard** that flicks its tongue to catch the spider

that spins its web to trap the bug
that sits on a leaf and nibbles the flower
that starts to bloom as it grows on the tree
that uses the light from the Sun to make its own food.

This is the **snake** that snaps its jaws to grab the lizard

that flicks its tongue to catch the spider
that spins its web to trap the bug
that sits on a leaf and nibbles the flower
that starts to bloom as it grows on the tree
that uses the light from the Sun to make its own food.

This is the **fox** that sneaks on its paws to pounce on the snake

that snaps its jaws to grab the lizard
that flicks its tongue to catch the spider
that spins its web to trap the bug
that sits on a leaf and nibbles the flower
that starts to bloom as it grows on the tree
that uses the light from the Sun to make its own food.

This is the **scat** that falls to the ground at the feet of the fox

that sneaks on its paws to pounce on the snake
that snaps its jaws to grab the lizard
that flicks its tongue to catch the spider
that spins its web to trap the bug
that sits on a leaf and nibbles the flower
that starts to bloom as it grows on the tree
that uses the light from the Sun to make its own food.

This is the **seed** that comes from the tree and lands in the scat

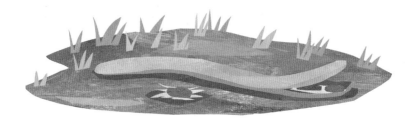

that falls to the ground at the feet of the fox
that sneaks on its paws to pounce on the snake
that snaps its jaws to grab the lizard
that flicks its tongue to catch the spider
that spins its web to trap the bug
that sits on a leaf and nibbles the flower
that starts to bloom as it grows on the tree
that uses the light from the Sun to make its own food.

This is the **sprout**
that grows from the seed
and reaches toward the Sun...

and this is the **Sun**
that brings the circle to life.

This Is the Sun / Este es el Sol [reversible edition]
Bilingual Hardback first edition • August 2023 • ISBN: 978-1-958629-26-0
Bilingual Paperback first edition • August 2023 • ISBN: 978-1-958629-19-2

Written by Elizabeth Everett, Text © 2022, 2023
Illustrated by Evelline Andrya, Illustrations © 2022, 2023

Project Manager, Cover and Book Design: Caitlin Burnham
Reversible Book Design: Hannah Thelen
Editors: Marlee Brooks, Hannah Thelen
Translator: Pilar Suescum
Spanish-Language Editor: Andrea Batista

Also available:
English Hardcover first edition • October 2022 • ISBN: 978-1-938492-81-5
English Paperback first edition • October 2022 • ISBN: 978-1-938492-82-2
English eBook first edition • October 2022 • ISBN: 978-1-938492-83-9
Spanish Paperback first edition • October 2022 • ISBN: 978-1-938492-84-6
Spanish eBook first edition • October 2022 • ISBN: 978-1-938492-85-3

Teacher's Guide available at the Educational Resources page of ScienceNaturally.com.

Published by:
Science, Naturally! – An imprint of Platypus Media, LLC
750 First Street NE, Suite 700
Washington, DC 20002
202-465-4798 • Fax: 202-558-2132
Info@ScienceNaturally.com • ScienceNaturally.com

Distributed to the book trade by:
National Book Network (North America)
301-459-3366 • Toll-free: 800-462-6420
CustomerCare@NBNbooks.com • NBNbooks.com
NBN International (worldwide)
NBNi.Cservs@IngramContent.com • Distribution.NBNi.co.uk

Library of Congress Control Number: 2022948453

10 9 8 7 6 5 4 3 2 1

Printed in China.